Contents

Editorial

Higher Aim

Prashant Trivedi aka PT, explains what the human body is for and how it is meant to be used on this earth.

In this time of Covid-19 panic & upheaval, PT offers a PaTh of hoPe, Peace, joy, higher evolution, & ultimate freedom.

Welcome to the very first issue of The Avatar Tribune

This magazine provides latest news & updates on **Prashant Trivedi** aka **PT, the Avatar for this Age of Aquarius.**

Every 2000 years we enter a New Age, a calculation based on the earth's axial precession. Our transition into the Age of Aquarius has been gaining momentum in the last two decades, especially since the appearance of internet making gnowledge more & more accessible to the wider public.

Every new Age of humanity brings with it a new Avatar, an incarnation of Divine will, a beacon of spiritual inspiration and enlightenment. The Avatar is always the initiator of real change when He appears.

Since he has been on this earth PT has changed the lives of many. His PasTimes are unique & his wisdom is always the best source of gnowledge available. **The Avatar Tribune** strives to PresenT & Praise **PT** & his activities in the best way it can.

4

AVATAR

"**Avatar** in Sanskrit means crossing over/ "You cross over" .

There are many Purposes to an Avatar.

For examPle if an Avatar comes down they are there to raise Bhudevi's
vibrations uP. That is one of the Purposes, to save
Bhu- Devi (mother earth) & to set up standards
and PrecedenTs for PhuTure times.

Still the most imPorTant reason is to actually save the sPiriTs
& give them an oPporTunity to get out of the
physical realm of existence. That is the main Purpose.

Avatar is coming from the Divine realm, coming back into the Physical,
& is like everybody else when they are here except
Avatar goes into the Prison of their own accord.

Normal sPiriTs when they are born into this Prison, they do that because
they have no other oPTion, because they are caught in the
cycle of birth & death. They don't have enough gnowledge or
energy to get out of the 3D existence into other realms. When
Divine makes that journey, it is done through one's
own will and choice. " - PT

Latest News

Crop Circles season is on !
Celestial SignPosTs

Elementals are stamping messages for humanity to pay attention to. Find the main happening of this season, its meaning and more.

PT sPeaks –
Predictions, Clarifications, Revelations

PT gives true wisdom for the benefit of all humanity. PT clarifies misconceptions and gives true gems of gnowledge about divinity and society

P's giTa
The most imPorTant book of the PlaneT
Buy now – in 11 languages

Kalki - Return of the Birdman
Sonics for the 21st Century

BeOmega made an enormous come back on 4th July 2021 with their new album "Kalki – Return of the Birdman". Learn about true music and sound science.

Announcement
Out Now
Avatar Walks the Earth
Praise Songs To Divine

Avatar Walks The Earth

Nav = 9 VraTi = Night   Oct 2021

Navratri is a sPecial time of year that has been celebrated since ancient times. It is still acknowledged in India but in the present day has been reduced to a superficial festival to honor the goddess Durga without understanding the real significance behind such worship. PT exPlains the deePer meaning of Navatri time and what it really rePresenTs.

Navratri happens twice a year. PT exPlains this is the time when the balance in nature is PerfecT. During Navratri, the Sun and the Moon are both at medium Power. Sun is strong in summer and weak in winter and reaches middle Power during sPring and autumn exPlaining why Navratri happens twice a year.

Everything in the universe functions on the basis of the masculine and the feminine. The Solar PrinciPle relates to the masculine (father etc) and the Lunar PrinciPle relates to the feminine (mother etc).

The Moon waxes and wanes towards a full Moon and a new Moon every 15 days. As a consequence, an entire lunar cycle lasts for 30 days. PT PoinTs out that this is why the word "month" finds its root in the word "Moon".

During the 9th day of the waxing cycle, the Moon is considered balanced, not full nor new. This is when the Moon is at medium Power.

As a result, when the Sun is at medium Power (spring and autumn) and the Moon reaches the 9th day of the waxing cycle that month, this is the time when the whole earth is in PerfecT balance as the solar and the lunar principle are the basis on which all functions on this Plane.

7

"in the environment around us on earth, this balance happens twice a year" - PT

This is therefore a crucial time for every living entity on earth and has to be utilized properly. Just like nature, the human body is also based on the solar and lunar principle. PT has often highlighted the importance of centering oneself and connecting with nature on a regular basis. It is only normal to align with the functioning of one's body when aspiring for any kind of well-being/happiness.

PT declares that the 9 nights of Navratri are meant to be used to build up to a perfect centering culminating on the 9th night when PerfecT balance happens. PT coherently insists on the fact that there has to be a center inside and outside which makes for a very powerful time.

One can get help with their centering during these times as PT has musical Plays for each of the 9 Navratri nights. Each night will carry a different

energy and listening to these Plays with receptive ears will help one align one's vibrations with the vibrations of divine & nature. PT's Plays are made during sunset time when the energy of the sun and the moon are in balance as well.

Navratri is celebrated at night as it is also seen at the time where goddess Durga won over the demons. In other words, it is victory of good over evil. In Practical terms, the victory over negative forces happens because of centering.

Centering should always lead one to honor PT the Axis, the one who brought back centering and teaches Pure PrinciPles.

This year's Autumn Navratri runs from 7th October to 15th October.

PT

aka

Prashant Trivedi

Considered by many to be the world's foremost authority on Jyotish & Vedic wisdom, **PT** is the leader of a Vedic revolution on this Earth.

He hails from an ancestry of notable Sanskrit scholars, writers, astrologers and Ayurvedic practitioners and was surrounded by ancient vedic mythology & cosmology from a very young age.

After completing his IIT degree, he received an invitation to undertake a spiritual pilgrimage to meet the Elders of the Hopi native American Indian tribe of Arizona. His time with the Hopi Elders was of deep collective significance & heralded new times for this Plane-T.

"The actual ancient Vedic way is a scientific way. Right now Science has reached that level where it can validate that way being the correct way, or being the only way one can live and die successfully." - PT

"Actual Sanskrit ~ Pra-shant = (Pra) Very (Shant) Peaceful
Tri-vedi = 3 Vedas or 3 main systems of knowledge "

Over the last 20 years PT 's footsteps have graced every corner of Mother Earth, honoring her & spreading his sonic healing musical vibrations.

He has been teaching the importance of approaching Vedic science in the way it was originally intended.

He is here to help us develop an honest foundation, something that needs to be introduced back into the world of Vedic Astrology and modern spiritual teachings.

PT 's PracTicality is unmatched as he not only reminds us of the forgotten Timeless Laws of this Multiverse but he is a true embodiment of them. He walks the talk and is able to live in harmony with divine and nature. He teaches about it to whoever is willing to learn.

He founded - Orion School & Foundation for Astrology in 2000. His astrological works are recognized by experts around the world to be the most indePTh on highly inscrutable topics such as lunar nodes and nakshatras. These books are part of an essential library for vedic astrologers and include "The Key of Life - Astrology of the Lunar Nodes", "Sun, The

Cosmic Powerhouse", "The 27 Celestial Portals" (aka "The Book of Nakshatras").

PT has appeared on numerous media outlets including online, British & US radio & television, Indian & Nepalese television & has been a speaker at international events and festivals.

> "everything is not God. There is a 'moving away from God' and that's why there is 'pain' " - PT

He has performed on musical stages in New York & London, having released his debut album "Outer Edge of Musiverse" under the band name BeOmega (2004). He came back with lightning prophetic sounds on his new album "Kalki - Return of the Birdman" in July 2021.

His free Sonic Plays & film archives can be experienced at Lotus Ocean (You Tube).

PT receives unique responses from nature including croP circle Phenomena & Rainbow ResPonses. There are hundreds of these documented responses at "Lotus Ocean" You Tube Channel. PT's teachings bring an awareness of reality which is rarely touched uPon in newage, religious, spiritual communities.

He has Published "P's giTa", a new ScriPTure for these times.

Available now in 11 languages, these teachings are essential Truths for anybody interested in their sPiriTual evolution.

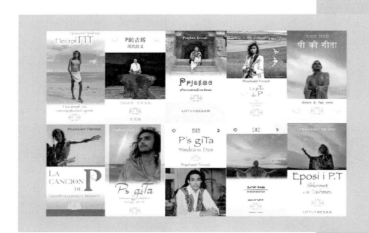

P's gita - Scriptures for the Now

is available at
www.lotus-ocean.net

& selected online retailers including Amazon, Abe Books & Waterstones.

Hear PT sPeaks
on the world wide web

PT sPeaks you tube channel

PT sPeaks is at radio republic.com

PT sPeaks is at sPoTify

PT sPeaks is at listennotes.com

PT sPeaks is at apple.com

PT sPeaks "Real Name of God Revealed"

The word "God" is seen and heard everywhere and every day. However, its true meaning is still not clear for most beings even to this day. The many different beliefs in the different religions of today are a perfect testimonial to that PhacT. Despite so many claiming to believe in God, no one has been able to explain God as clearly as PT did in a recent talk.

PT has often stated that "word makes the world" which PoinTs to a need to analyze the structure of words to understand their true core meanings. He explains that the terms "God" and "Divine" are full of misconceptions in the sense that they are vague terms and can be interpreted in many ways.

For starters, the term "God" refers to masculine only and the suPreme Phorce of the universe is beyond genders. PT clarifies that the term "God" means "Generator-Operator-Destroyer" and refers to the 3 vedic deities "Brahma, Vishnu and Shiv". In Vedic stories, the mention of "gods", "demi-gods" and "goddesses" is not a rare instance as the events recounted in these stories are not only referring to what happens on earthly planes but also higher and lower planes. This is an imPorTant PhacT to mention since the term God is often being used other than for designating the suPreme Phorce of the universe and creates confusion around what that term truly refers to.

"ParamaTman means PerfecT coherence, PerfecT PhracTal... the word PerfecT relates to ParamaTman"

"You can make a lot of gods but ParamaTman will remain the same"

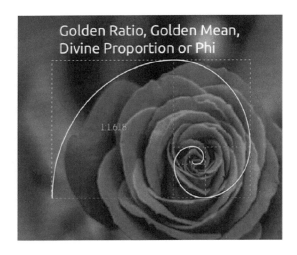

Golden Ratio, Golden Mean, Divine Proportion or Phi

1:1.618

PT declares that the English language doesn't have a term that captures the true essence of the suPreme Phorce of the multiverse.

This is where he brings up the Sanskrit term "ParamaTman". This term is related to the word "atma" meaning "self". All beings have an atma. The closest equivalent to "atma" in English language is "spirit". PT says that the atma is different in every being and has different levels. ParamaTman is the highest level or what people call God.

Just as atma can take form on earth, ParamaTman is also capable of doing so. Whatever any atma can do, ParamaTman can do since it is PerfecTion or what P refers to as PerfecT PhracTality/Coherence.

All atma are not equal. There is a difference of spirit in everybody, which is what gives room for evolution. PT says that all beings have a different level of coherence which makes each person different.

Even though atma ('sPirit') doesn't die, it is limited, whilst ParamaTman is unlimited. PT exPlains that ParamaTman is the biggest PhracTal and atma is a smaller Phractal connected to it. The terms "ParamaTman" and "atma" help to understand the difference that exists between all beings and PerfecTion (God). It also highlights the PhacT that no one is equal.

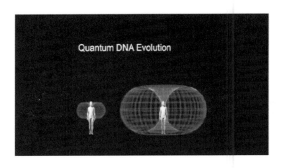

Quantum DNA Evolution

PT's scientific definitions clarify not only the name of God, but also our PosiTion in reference to that suPreme Phorce which leads to true understanding of the self.

For full talk visit
You Tube channel - **PT sPeaks**
"Real Name of 'God' Revealed"

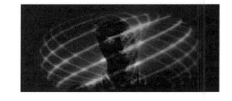

PT sPeaks on 'cult' & 'culture'

You Tube Channel - PT sPeaks May 2021

"The root of the word "cult" is "culture" says PT. The word "cult" is a big word in the west which has rendered the meaning of "culture" to be misunderstood. "Cult" is simPly "culture" without the "ure".

PT brings up the question : "Why would someone want to create this word?". He declares that there are beings who are afraid of Real Culture. Indeed, the beings who are running society, the main stream society are making sure that it lacks culture. PT makes it clear that culture is enriching. It is useful. It evolves oneself. On the other hand, the word cult has a negative connotation. PT exPlains that since the beings in control are afraid of culture coming out, they have cut the word "culture" in half to create the term "cult". Besides that, they have created groups that have been seen in a negative light so that the term "cult" becomes a bad thing in the eyes of the public.

"It is a very thought out thing to create this fear about this word so that people are afraid to step out into any kind of group. Group always has more influence than one person. A group can attract more people than one person. So to stop that from happening, from independent groups of any kind being form, this term was made up." says PT.

PT says that those in control have given the false impression that everything outside the mainstream media is mad and crazy.

This programming is especially in place in the west. Whenever there is a new group

19

that are not necessarily understood, that is outside of the mainstream, they are mindlessly labelled as a cult. PT gives a PracTical example. He exPlains that if everybody in society is eating meat and doing so is the norm, it is ok in everyone's eyes. In reality however, eating meat should be seen as a cult because it is taking beings down the path of devolution. However, if some other being comes from outside society and introduces a vegetarian diet whereby people start adopting this diet, these people will then be labelled a cult, even though teachings about vegetarianism used to be passed down from generation to generation in many parts of the world and this behavior is much more to do with true culture.

As PT aptly says, *"Everything might be going bad within the system. Everybody might be suffering but there is no problem with that, no problem at all. People's diseases might be rising. People's mental condition might be getting worse. Every possible negative thing might be happening, wars on top of it and a hundred thousand addictions... But that is all ok, that is not a cult."*

"Vedic culture unites everyone" PT

PT insists on the PhacT that this word "cult" had to be created because some behind-the-scenes people are very scared of real culture sPreading in society. Otherwise, there would be no need to literally cut "culture" in half. If culture sPreads, the sheep will get out of the boundaries that the mainstream have set up for them. Most people remain attached to the system even though it creates constant pain of all kinds, whether mental, physical or otherwise. This system is set up so that people are afraid of stepping out into other groups that can have influence.

PT also PoinTs out that the objectives of society are not even gnown to those who tirelessly work in it. What is the objective of following such ways? Most keep at it despite the clearly devolving implications of the mainstream ways of living ie. going to Macdonalds. sitting in any posture etc Whoever controls the media controls the mind and whoever is trying to educate themselves with culture and therefore trying to wash their mind from this programming are never seen in a good light. They are called "brain-washed". PT again brings some natural sense by saying that the brain needs some washing since it has been poisoned with so much nonsense from the media. PT says that what is labelled as good is actually bad and vice versa, since culture is often labelled as a cult and that what constitutes mainstream is seen as being completely normal despite its obvious devolving implications.

PT exPlains that true culture is based on true experience and not on blind belief. The mainstream broadcasts a lot of things as news or as PhacTs in the field of science or in other fields which have no way of being proven. The masses blindly 'believe' without any true empirical evidence and this is the real cult. There is a combination of a lack of purpose and of blind beliefs which makes people misunderstand what is what. PT clarifies ,
"I'm not saying that there aren't lots of groups that are not crazy. I'm not defending here in any way, shape or form but i'm just saying that for the mainstream to say anything, that's a big joke. There is a very big cult out there which is hiding culture from people, that's the actual situation, it's simple. "

20

PT also sPeaks of the many organisations including companies which have unwholesome purposes, and of their illogical validity in the eyes of the system and of the people. He cleverly and simPly PoinTs out the level of absurdity reached by mankind. When it comes to being presented with something bad such as cola drinks, they are instead seen as something good and completely normal. The amount of lies sPread by the system in the name of education, science, religion or other is ridiculously high. In the same way that the system makes people believe what cult is and what culture is, they also determine what is truth and what are lies in the eyes of the masses. People who get fooled by these terms will fall for the cliches deliberately propagated by the system rather than try to understand the true nature of reality.

PT says that one should go towards culture in the sense that it brings one closer to reality, and that the word cult is given by the system to those who are not wanting to change so that they can point fingers at those who are trying to evolve. The system wants to create a sense of pressure on those who want to step out of it. The purpose of this is to dissuade people from truly evolving.

PT also Points out other word transformations that are meant to manipulate our understanding such as "popular" becoming "pop". Visit lotus-ocean.net for PT's Plog titled "words".

PT adds that the ancient true vedic way of learning, which happens through the

guru-disciple relationship would be seen as a cult nowadays, as it differs so much from the thinking of the masses.

This is a great PoinT as today's education where people receive a lot of false info fits more into the definition of a cult. The bottom line is that in the mainstream system no true gnowledge can be passed down from one being to another until whoever is in control says so.

PT adds that humans beings have to decide whether they want to learn something

21

for themselves or not. Beings have to want their well-being. Otherwise the possibility of getting caught in these false notions becomes a danger and basically cuts off one's PhuTure development and evolution.

We are in the age of Aquarius and it is normal for beings to come together in groups as Aquarius is the 11th sign of the zodiac. Aquarius relates to the 11th house in a horoscope which is about groups.

PT reminds us that human beings are here to evolve and that if they decide to get together as a group in order to do so, nothing can stop them, not even labelling them as something they are not.

In this Age of Aquarius the "11" signification shows how society is meant to evolve ie. around a wise and capable leader that gnos about liPhe, the Aquarian leader who brings the true heavenly waters on to the thirsty populace.

The number of people waking up today is growing. Beings are realizing that they should not pay attention to the mainstream media as much as they used to.

PT rightfully highlights the PhacT that it is important to sPeak of these things because nobody else will. This is is probably the only talk on a toPic of this kind even though we are in 2021.

PT's unbreakable center is always admirable and he always stands in sPoTless integrity. He is able to guide people in the ancient Vedic way despite society being upside down. Truly Avataric.

Age of Aquarius

PT the Axis

Sound

KALKI
RETURN OF THE
BIRDMAN

Kalki - Return of the Birdman
Sonics for the 21st Century

"**Every town looks the same
Concrete cannot hide the pain
All fed up they walk the line
Long time before they saw this sign**

**Return of the Birdman
Return of the Birdman...**"

These are Powerful opening lines from **BeOmega's** latest album **"Kalki - Return of the Birdman"** which came out to rock the world's ears on 4th July 2021. This is the followup to their debut album **"Outer Edge of Musiverse"** which saw a re-release in 2020.

The liveliness of sonics on **"Kalki - Return of the Birdman"** are beyond words. With his band **BeOmega, PT** not only redefines what music is but what it probably should be.

Labyrinth like textures, compelling moods and a mysterious depth flowing from one track to the other can only be described as "god-given", as one feels themself getting embraced by a true sense of wholeness.

A steady foundational drum/bass and catchy electric guitar progression provides the PerfecT platform for the stylistic vocal of the anthemic **"Return of the Birdman"**. This contrasts nicely with the immersive experience of **"Venus"** which contrasts nicely with the harmonically seamless transcendental **"Magic Lake".**

PT is gnown to create sonics that influence the electromagnetic field of the earth. This album is not only nourishing for living entities on the PlaneT, it is rock n roll with an evolutionary edge. One gets to enjoy the depth of a highly developed consciousness driving every note, chord, strum & syllable. Rich in tonal quality, the sound of the album is healing, yet rocking, yet soothing, yet hard, yet soft. In addition the exclusive use of analog sounds offers the listener a more enriching experience.

Qualifying this album as PropheTic is a PhacT as **PT** declares "It gives the whole PicTure."

BeOmega burst onto the streaming scene in 2004. You won't find them peforming at conventional concerts, but rather playing "in Crop Circles that appear around Wiltshire, UK".

The 11 tracks of the album refer to the Aquarian hero aspect of frontman PT. The Birdman in the title is an Aquarian figure. The true Aquarian archetype stands on his own and is wholly self-reliant. The more esoteric aspect of this sign refers to the 'Savior of humanity' where the Aquarian hero brings the waters of liPhe to the people in need. Both the words "Birdman" and "Kalki" are directly connected to the archetype PT embodies.

1. Kalki - Return of the Birdman 3.27

2. Fly By 4.14

3. Venus 3.21

4. 21st Century 4.14

5. Waves of Charge 4.24

6. Children of the Night 8.38

7. Kalki Avatar is Here 4.56

8. The Sword 7.17

9. PT Charge 6.06

10. ArdraRudra Cleansing 5.19

11. Magic Lake 3.03

PT's sonics are magickally multi-layered and often reveal much more than words can tell.

The trancendental stories of the lord are expressed through the Avatar's voice & guitar.

It is up to us to learn to appreciate them for what they truly are.

Lotus Ocean Music

You Tube

PT sonics, unlike most mainstream music, are created on the sPoT and carry a truly sPonTaneous signature. PT describes his music as a way for him to relate to the natural environment. Being a Phully PhracTal and coherent being, it is only logical that PT's music raises the vibrations of whoever gets a chance to listen to it. This music is very different to whatever is produced by the mainstream. It usually takes time for the listener to acclimatize to PT's unique sounds. Nevertheless, once one gives it time and is able to surrender to PT's pace, one begins to feel an effortless guidance into deep healing vibrations. The vast output of sounds that PT generously shares is truly consciousness expanding and one can literally exPerience vibrations from another world. The PhacT that PT's vibrational field is so much higher, is what makes it hard for the listener to go back to other music. His sonics are wholly Phun, creative and deep which makes for new Profound experiences every time. One can draw on a new sense of Phreedom from these sounds because PT's music doesn't follow regular patterns, his style, tones, colors, moods are always changing. PT's unmatched sPontaneity is also seen by the PhacT that most of his songs don't have fixed notes. His songs are never rigid and Phlow effortlessly with the natural vibe around him. His Plays can be fast, slow, soft, hard, sweet, rocking. They truly can be anything.

"Sound can be used to play and interact with elements of nature. If you do a particular kind of sound then a lightning storm will happen or if you do a particular kind of sound rain will happen .

Music is for interaction with elements and people forget that in this day and age because for people today music is something else. People's music is usually about dealing with other people. It's nothing about dealing with the elements of nature anymore." - PT

In real Dhanishta fashion (Dhanishta is one of the 27 constellations of the zodiac that PT writes about in his book "The 27 Celestial PorTals"), PT's sense of rhythm is captivating and hypnotic to listen to.

The most sPecTacular evidence of PT's musical suPerioriTy is the PhacT that nature resPonds to his sounds. Whether the resPonse manifests as a rainbow, lightning, rain or something else, it is a unique signature of PT's that pushes the envelop of what music is. PT describes this Phenomenon as "bio-feedback" and has talked about it in some depth on many occasions. He specifies that sound can be used to play and interact with the elements of nature. A particular type of sound will trigger a lightning storm to happen where as another type of sound will make rain fall. PT explains that sound is a complex science and PT has been a testimony to that PhacT for decades. In today's day and age, people have lost touch with nature and are not aware of its intrinsic connection with music. PT describes an ancient time where music was primarily used to connect with the elements ie. earth, water, Phire, air and sky. This is what LotusOcean music is about ie. connecting the 5 elements of the human body with the same 5 elements existing in nature through a musical 'instrument' which can also be called 'yantra'. This is a very new usage of the term 'yantra' that helps to give it a living dynamic identity.

PT states that the more connected to Divine one is, the more coherent one is, the more one can interact with nature and sound, which is what PT does on a regular basis.

"As inside, so outside"
PT's beauty is freely expressed in the earth skies.

28

BEST TONES ON THE PLANET

In this You Tube channel, PT exPlores tube amplifiers dating specifically from the 30's to the 60's . PT is a true sound exPerT and exPerimenTer. He exPlains that tube amps made during these times Produced sounds that were more rich, more complex and more warm than their present day counterpart. Besides this their tones are much healthier. They have true soul-stirring potential when played by PT.

PT's favorite instrument is the electric guitar and for good reasons. Among instruments, electric guitars are capable of covering the largest number of sounds, tones and frequencies. As implied in its name electric guitar is electrical equipment . Like wise , the human body is electrical equipment. It is because of this that the player is able to convey his vibrations through the instrument and affect other beings on an actual spirit level. It is for this reason that PT has always emphasized that this is not an instrument for just anyone and should be used by the wise only.

For a real listening experience in electric guitar "Games of Tones - Best Tones on the PlaneT" channel is a tremendous opportunity to exPerience PT's vast, mysterious and enchanting world.

"The Divine comes down sim Ply to Play
& see who is willing to Play " - PT

Light

Turquoise PhracTality

RAINBOW PHRACTALITY

PT 's Rainbow Steps light up the Forest

Once upon a time
a man so refined
brought to earth his charms
from far beyond the stars

Crop Circles

Crop Circles or crop designs as far as history recalls, started to appear regularly since 1975 which is PT's birth year. His Presence on earth has been attracting otherwordly forces which have stamped their symbolic messages to humanity in fields. Crop Circles have been happening in snow as well. They are present all over the world but happen mostly in England where PT lives. Even though they remain ungnown to most or very mysterious to those who come to gno about them, Crop Circles are documented and deciPhered every year on PT's You Tube channel **LotusOcean**.

The origins of Crop Circles cannot be human since past footage has proven that they are created in the blink of an eye. The designs are extremely Precise and would demand considerable time and effort for a human to even reproduce one on a piece of paper. The size of the design can vary but often covers a huge area |(several hundred feet sometimes) and none of the crops are broken or damaged. The stalks are folded to create complex geometrical patterns.

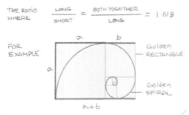

THE GOLDEN RATIO
PLEASING PROPORTIONS FOUND IN NATURE

THE RATIO WHERE $\frac{LONG}{SHORT} = \frac{BOTH\ TOGETHER}{LONG} = 1.618$

FOR EXAMPLE — Golden RECTANGLE — Golden SPIRAL

Crop Circles are an inter-dimensional Phenomenon. PT has exPlained that they are created by elementals, the forces of nature. Nature is based on Phi-Ratio and therefore only resPonds to a certain level of coherence. In other words, Crop Circles will reflect fractal coherence and Pure intents only. Over the years, PT has had hundreds of crop circle resPonses to his activities. This is incontestable proof of PT's suPerior level of coherence as Crop Circles are appearing every year and mirroring a lot of his personal life as it unfolds. The Crop Circles are consistently highlighting PT's collective importance in these times.

🕉 is the vedic symbol of creation and according to PT incompletely portrayed as "Om". PT has PoinTed out many times that the true sound associated with this symbol was not gnown. That was until PT did a chant the 6th of July 2007 in a cave gnown as West Kennet Longbarrow near Silbury Hill in the south of England. The next day, the crop circle below appeared 5 miles away from the cave revealing the true sound of creation on a giant canvas of 1000 yards square.

Aeioum Crop Circle

Lotus Ocean You Tube Channel
"CropCircle on 7.7.7 ~ Prashant Trivedi"

PT's Chanting "Aeioum"

Exactly 14 years later on 7-7-21, PT plays in this bullseye crop circle

Lotus Ocean You Tube Channel (Trailer)
"7 7 7 to 7 7 21 - PT's Crop Circle Saga Play"

One can watch the full Video at Lotus Ocean Patreon Channel

The Sudarshan Crop Circle Series

The 7-7-7 Aeioum Crop Circle marked the beginning of PT's ongoing Crop Circle Saga ...

On the 21st June 2020, a series of similar crop circles have started to appear. Their designs clearly depict Sudarshan Chakras, the Weapon of Narayan.

Su = Good – Darshan = Vision

Even though crop circle designs of Sudarshan Chakras have happened in the past, they have never appeared repeatedly in this way before. The years of 2020 & 2021 have been filled with Sudarshan Chakra resPonses. They evidently refer to the Avatar's Presence on earth, as this continuous stamping of Sudarshan Chakras can only refer to Vishnu's current incarnation. Lord Vishnu is often depicted holding the Sudarshan Chakra on his right index finger. In Vedic texts the Sudarshan Chakra is described to be the strongest weapon in the world. 2020 and 2021 crop circle resPonses are PoinTing to the PoTency of PT's Presence on earth even more than before. There have been more than 20 Sudarshan Chakra resPonses to PT's plays and activities from the 21st June 2021 up till now.

You Tube Channel - Lotus Ocean
"Crop Circle resPonse to PT's Crop Circle Play on 13th July 2020"

39

PT's declaration on the 13th July 2020 during a crop circle concert triggered many resPonses over the last year. The Celestial Time Discus/Sudarshan Chakra refers to the Sustainer's effortless ability to bring balance in the multiverse through the inherent suPerior PhracTaliTy of his all-Pervading Self. The Sudarshan Chakra symbolizes the PhacT that Vishnu is not just undefeatable, he also monitors the state of the world. The Avatar's Sudarshan Chakra also represents the wheel of time and is gnown to have cut the heads off those who refused to align with the Divine will. All these asPecTs make sense in relation to PT's activities.

Most people gno that the year 2020 has been crucial in many regards. Those who have been following PT gno that it is a year of Judgement as the number 20 in numerological terms refers to the Judgement itself. The strong Presence of the Avatar's weapon depicted in crop circles is a testimonial for what is truly happening on earth. It is time for all beings to realign with the divine will before it is too late.

You Tube Channel - Lotus Ocean
"the alPha and the omega" (trailer)
full video on Lotus Ocean PaTreon

The AlPha & Omega

On the 24th June 2021, PT does a declaration in a sudarshan chakra crop circle. This Play was uploaded on the 18th July 2021 on PT's Patreon. The same day of the uPload in the same area (hamPshire, England), the crop circle below appeared matching PT's Play.

40

The letter "A" for alPha and the greek symbol Ω for omega are visible in this design. The connection is clear. This is not the only imPorTant symbolism in this crop circle which PT Precisely illustrates in his video.

Two days later, the crop circle below appeared in hamPshire as well. The letter "A" for alPha is visible again and the letter "O" for omega is there as well.

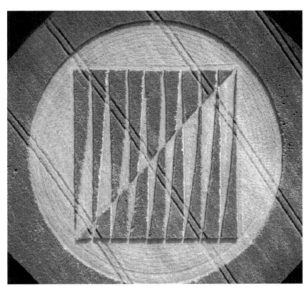  

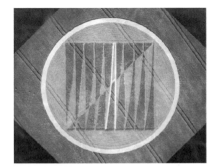

One can notice the lightning symbol in this crop circle also. It is interesting to gno that there was a lightning symbol on PT's amp during another crop circle declaration that happened on the 22nd of July 2021.

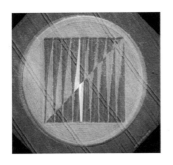

the same exact lightning electric symbol !!

Crop Circles are always Pointing towards
PT

Real Vedic Astrology
with PT

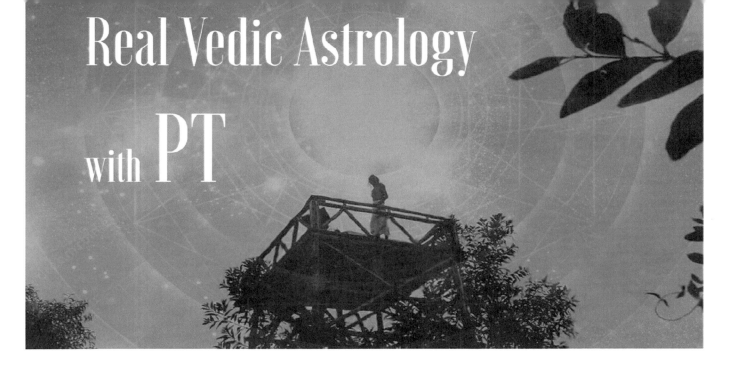

PT is recognized by many to be the real authority on Vedic science. His understanding of life is Profound. This PhacT is highly supported by his unmatched wisdom in the complex science of Jyotish (Vedic Astrology). His books on this toPic have comPleTely changed this field and no student of Jyotish can afford to miss out on PT's Jyotish masterpieces. The following talk in London is a fine example of PT's acumen.

PT's astrology PredicTions from 3rd November 2019 are Coming True Right Now .. YOU TUBE CHANNEL - PT SPEAKS

PT sPeaks at the Theosophical Society of London 3 November 2019
about the stars as they align from dec 2019 to 2020 and onwards from a Jyotish
(Vedic astrology) PersPecTive

Saturn conjunct Jupiter in Capricorn Transit
30th March to 1st July 2020
& 15th September to 21st November 2021

Jupiter and Saturn were conjunct in the sign of Capricorn from 30th March to 1st July 2020 and this conjunction occurs again when Jupiter moves retrograde from Aquarius back into Capricorn from 15th September to 21st November 2021.

"You will see a complete Paradigm shift," said PT about these 2 grahas (celestial bodies) Jupiter and Saturn coming together. Jupiter and Saturn are both connected to the law. PT explained that the sign Capricorn gives this transit an emphasis on the system as Capricorn is related to the system - *"Capricorn is the matrix."*

PT was spot on when he declared, *"The whole political system, the social political system, the TRUTH about it will be revealed to the masses."* The Covid - 19 chaos that started in 2020 is the best testimonial to that PhacT.

"All the trade laws and all the laws will undergo a shift while Saturn is in Capricorn." -PT

It is amazing to see how PT's words are coming true like the words of a rishi from olden times. He stated that beings would have to make a choice regarding whether they believe in man-made laws or multiversal/universal laws.

He raised the question, *"How much sense do man made laws around the world make?"* The focus will have to shift because manmade laws are not working. They are only oppressive and people all over the world are not happy with them.

"If the laws become more draconian as they are trying to do then masses will obviously fight back."-PT

Once again we see PT's words in action as beings all around the world are protesting against the different measures taken by the government whether it be lockdowns, vaccines or other.

PT went on further, *"If the manmade laws are not aligning with the universal laws, those laws have no meaning and they only bring you down."*

The whole masses needs to decide on whether or not they are satisfied with whatever laws are enforced right now in the world. The transitting influence of Saturn helps by giving a sense of restriction and puts current laws into serious questioning.

PT also explained that most beings don't even think in terms of multiversal laws. He stated that any construct has to have some laws, which is why this earth we live on has to have some some laws that need to be followed. PT insists on the PhacT that there is no going past multiversal laws as they are timeless and much more important than manmade laws. Because manmade laws are oppressive PT says it is actually easier for all beings to align with multiversal laws.

"It's a PhacT that these laws (Multiversal laws) exist and these laws are there. People will actually have to confront one thing now, masses as a whole, layman to layman, whether they believe in manmade laws or in the universal laws. There are two kinds of laws."-PT

Multiversal laws are explained with PerfecT Precision in **"P's giTa - ScriPTures for the now"**.

44

P's giTa - ScriPTures for the Now

Available at lotus-ocean.net

PT raised another very insightful PoinT regarding what he described as the internet generation. He explained that young people who are born with the internet (1995 onwards) will speak up during the Saturn - Jupiter conjunction period, which is something that we have witnessed already in many countries. PT explained that the reason for this is that the sense of law on the internet is very different compared to the sense of law that the government conveys. PT added that most laws are outdated and won't be tolerated in the PhuTure.

"You might even see a whole earth law as a whole all over the earth instead of country laws." - PT

This prediction has come true as nearly all countries have been under serious lockdown during 2020 till now.

PT described our times as a Paradigm shift and that this Saturn-Jupiter conjunction was a true turning point as the truth about the government keeps coming out.

It is no secret that PhacTs and truth have been hidden from people for a very long time especially in the last 100 years through propaganda, false news, programming etc. The internet has been a strong medium for

the truth to come out. PT declared that everyone can be a researcher, everyone can gno for themselves. People have access to much more information than they had 20 years ago.

Because human beings have free will they have created manmade laws which are very different to multiversal laws. This has created suffering due to people's own doing and all beings are getting the result of their own actions.

PT emphasized that the younger generation are less happy with the laws currently in place and once they start to gno about the real laws, they will start following them. He also stated that the system will undergo real change if the masses decide they want to follow the true multiversal laws.

PT declared that the system, the matrix, the government and the system that controls the government (all Capricorn related things) have to undergo a shift and the heavily controlled media will not be able to stop the truth from coming out like they have done in the past.

What will be considered mainstream in the future will be decided by the masses rather than by the government and media.

"People will make mainstream what they want to make mainstream rather than the media deciding or the government deciding. All of the control of the media and government is going to dissipate. PoinT is that people should come to gno the PhacTs and truths. People have to come to gno about the universal laws and then people can decide. That opportunity is there."-PT

JUPITER IN AQUARIUS BY PT

TALK MAY 2021
You Tube Channel - Madan Atriya

Jupiter transits Aquarius.
June 20th 2021 -
September 14th 2021

& re-enters Aquarius
from the sign
Capricorn
21st November 2021
to 13th April 2022

Jupiter and Saturn are no longer conjunct in the sky since Jupiter moved out of Capricorn and shifted into the sign of Aquarius. PT describes the shifting of Jupiter into Aquarius as a time commonly celebrated in India called Mahakumb, a festival that happens every 12 years. PT exPlains, *"Jupiter in Aquarius is nothing to do with a festival, it is to do with the energy of the sign Aquarius."*

Jupiter's sojourn into Aquarius occurs every 12 years as Jupiter takes around 1 year to transit a sign of the zodiac.

PT states that all Aquarian things such as technology, internet and sPiriTuality are rising in Prominence during this time. Jupiter is the guru and its energies are about teaching. The combining of its energy with the energy of Aquarius make room for the basic Principles of the Age of Aquarius to come about for the masses.

PT says, *"The basic principles have to be formulated right now and told to the masses."* These Principles are the absolute basic multiversal truths taught in Lotus Ocean by PT (The

46

Aquarian Avatar) himself.

PT says, *"There are basic principles to what should be human life and how human beings should live. What is a human being supposed to do? How are they suppose to behave? What should be their mentality? What should be their way of being? How to deal with your own self, your own body and how to deal with others? All these things within the Aquarian concept have to be taught. People are ready to receive these instructions."*

This gnowledge has already been formulated in **"P's giTa-ScriPTures for the Now"** and it is time for the gnowledge to be sPread.

PT says, *"The dissemination of this gnowledge is the main job in the whole year. Jupiter will facilitate that. The whole focus here is on learning after the initial shock (Co-vid 19 chaos). That is a positive energy and that will be the real MahaKumbh. It is deepening yourself in the river of gnowledge. Jupiter creates this environment where teaching is available. For those who are willing to learn, it's a very good time."*

PT explains that the learning needs to be PracTical and real as Saturn, the planet which represents reality rules the sign of Aquarius.

He states that the coming of Saturn in Aquarius later from 28th April 2022 to 29th March 2025 will bring some concretization to the learning that takes place when Jupiter is in Aquarius.

PT says, *"This is the ideal time where you have the time. Situation can be so bad at a different time that you won't have the time to learn. There is no harm in being afraid because being afraid should trigger you to learn. The fear has to be used positively for learning. It is another year of grace. Guru (Jupiter) is grace. Whatever is happening externally, you still have time and opportunity to learn.*

Available at
online stores
including
Amazon
Abe books
Waterstones

or Visit

lotus-ocean.net

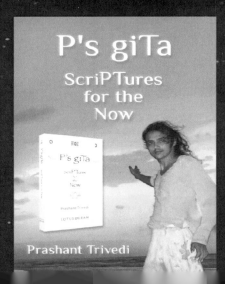

P's giTa
ScriPTures
for the
Now

Prashant Trivedi

If you don't learn and apply now, in the future things will get more tough and difficult. It's not going to get easier."

Lotus Ocean meditation classes are held online in different languages around the world. To attend a class one can visit Lotus Ocean Meditation on Facebook.

PT Series - Houses of the Zodiac

PT exPlains Things the way they are meant to be exPlained

You Tube Channel - Electrically Alkaline

You Tube Channel - Electrically Alkaline

"Prash Trivedi: The 1st House"

PT starts by exPlaining that the most important thing seen from the Ascendant or 1st House is the personality. Hence, the native will have the personality of whatever is rising on their Ascendant. PT PoinTs out that people have been ascribing the personality to the sun sign, especially in western astrology. Oftentimes, people say "I'm a Libra. You're Capricorn." etc. People have learnt the personality traits of these signs. "Whatever people learnt about sun signs, that will not go to waste if applied to this thing called the Ascendant," says PT.

PT first divides the signs into 4 types – air, fire, earth and water.The 1st house is going to have one of these 4 elements and that will tell a lot about the personality of the native.

PT further divides signs into 3 more groups - The cardinal or movable signs being the 1st, the 4th, the 7th and the 10 signs, the fixed signs being the 2nd, the 5th, the 8th and the 11th. Lastly comes the dual signs being the 3rd, the 6th, the 9th and the 12th. These 3 types of signs come on top of elemental classification.

The movable signs like to move, the fixed signs don't like much movement and dual signs like both in equal measure. As an example, Capricorn is an earth sign as well as a movable sign.

As a consequence, Capricorn moves only for practical purposes. When on the Ascendant this would define the personality of the native in great measure hence the Ascendant or 1st house is considered to be the basic core house.

The 1st house is the only house that is considered Kendra and Trikone at the same time.

House Categories	Houses include
Kendra houses	1st, 4th, 7th & 10th house
Trikona houses	1st, 5th & 9th house
Dusthana/ Triksthana houses	6th, 8th & 12th house
Trishadaya houses	3rd, 6th & 11th house
Upachaya houses	3rd, 6th, 10th & 11th house
Marakasthana houses	2nd & 7th house

PT states that the 1st house is the most auspicious house for any being. This is an important fact for any astrology student as this is often forgotten by astrologers even though it is crucial in any chart analysis. PT further exPlains that one comes on earth to evolve and that the 1st house of the physical body is the first platform for that.

PT also clarifies that the 1st house might have

50

"Your Ascendant is for life.
Nobody is going to turn from a
Capricorn to Libra later in life.
Nobody undergoes body
metamorphosis like that."

problems based on previous karm but it has to be used to take things forward and that no other house can have meaning without the 1st house. The 1st house along with the 1st lord has to be seen first in the horoscope before all else.

Taking the example of Aquarius rising, a sign ruled by Saturn, one has to look at where Saturn is in the chart. The placement of that graha becomes the most important thing in the native's life. PT gives the example of the 1st lord in the 3rd house where the 1st lord has gone into the house of short journeys and communication. Such person will never say no to short journeys and will always be up for communication, writing etc.

Also, what is in the 1st house influences the personality of the native. Whatever graha is there will be seen clearly in the native's personality.

Vedic Astrologers sometimes assign the 1st house of the Navamsa chart (a derivative chart of the main horoscope) as a replacement for the Ascendant or 1st house later in life. PT states that the Ascendant one is born with doesn't change and remains the Ascendant for life.

The Navamsa D9 chart divides each sign of the horoscope into 9 divisions and PT explains that it only shows which part of the sign one is born in. The D9 is applicable from the time one is born, but no being undergoes body changes because the Ascendant switches to another one. Body is one and doesn't become different because of Navamsa ascendant. Some changes are possible but the basic core remains the same.

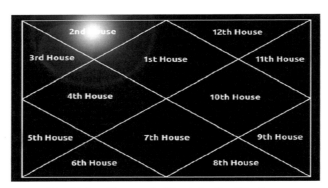

You Tube Channel - Electrically Alkaline

"Prash Trivedi: The 2nd House"

As PT has previously stated, the 1st house is the body and the self. He exPlains that the 2nd house is about one's surroundings.
"...the circumstances when you're born, those circumstances are 2nd house"
"whatever you can touch is your 2nd house".

It is about the nourishment one gets and what is around oneself. " He also says that in this day and age, the things around oneself cost money and is the reason why the 2nd house is referred to as the house of money. PT gets to a deeper root and describes it as the house of resources

"If your family has better values, you have a better 2nd house and you will get better food. If they don't you won't."

"What to eat is also gnowledge. What matters is what you eat. You might have millions of dollars but you might not gno what to eat."

"Gnowledge and 2nd house have an intimate connection."

directly around oneself which can include money. It is also the house of family as that is whatever is around oneself. It is also the house of childhood.

With regards to body parts, the 2nd house rules the face (eyes, mouth etc) as well as some part of the throat. Food is also related to the 2nd house, as it is something within one's reach. PT further exPlains that the values of one's family will determine the type of food one gets, as well as the type of gnowledge and values one is influenced by. This can all be seen from the 2nd house.

What one eats is much more important than how much money one has, and even the capability of understanding this PhacT has to do with one's 2nd house. 2nd house is also the house of gnowledge and sPeech. If one doesn't have gnowledge, one will speak nonsense and PT PoinTs out that all of this is greatly defined by the family one is born into.

For example, Rahu in the 2nd house will show that there is something strange in the family, childhood and surroundings. PT brilliantly PoinTs out that the 2nd house should always be seen as one's surroundings as whenever one gets gnowledge, the first thing one does is change their surroundings. Gnowledge and 2nd house have an intimate connection.

The 2nd house is an earthy house. It is a practical house to do with the senses. A lot of the sensations we get from the material world are related to this house. PT also states that it is not just the house of the senses but also the house of natural sense or common sense. He also brilliantly states that this earth is a big Plane but that the 2nd house has to do only with whatever is immediately around oneself. In other words, it is one's practical earthly surroundings.

This description of the 2nd house has never been given publicly before PT delivered this talk. It should be highlighted that all beings on this Plane can gain access to true gnowledge and true sense through PT's teachings and as a result can improve their 2nd house greatly.

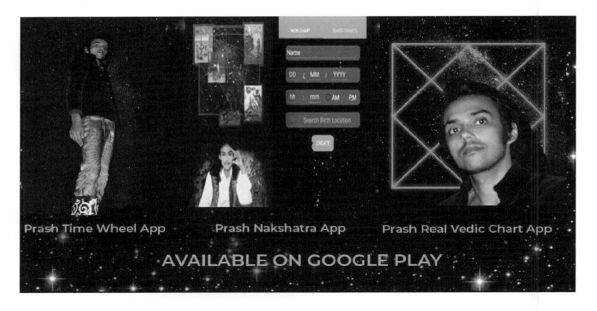

Prash Time Wheel App   Prash Nakshatra App   Prash Real Vedic Chart App

AVAILABLE ON GOOGLE PLAY

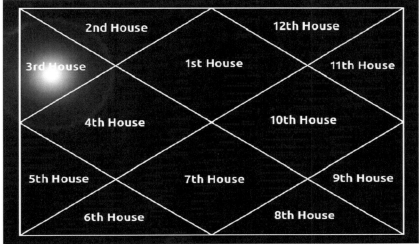

2nd House	12th House
3rd House	1st House	11th House
4th House	10th House
5th House	7th House	9th House
6th House	8th House

You Tube Channel - Electrically Alkaline

"Prash Trivedi: The Third House"

PT reminds us that the 3rd house comes after the 2nd house and that simPly gnowing that really helps understand the core meaning of the 3rd house. The 2nd house is responsible for the food we are able to eat to get energy. The use of that energy is the 3rd house.

PT adds that the 3rd house automatically becomes the house of courage since it is where any infant would begin their journey in life by starting to crawl after they've been fed. The 3rd house is related to short distance journeys. Moving from one place to another even in the same room as a baby would, is a short journey.

When babies start crawling it is also a time when they strive to start expressing themselves and thus 3rd house is also the house of communication. It is not only a baby's first steps, but also his first few words. When one is 2 years old (2nd house), one might say some words but at 3 years old (3rd house) one starts to put sentences together.

PT says, "Third house is the first house of the outflow of energy." One is born in the 1st house. The 2nd house is where one is getting nourished and the 3rd house is where one is using that energy for the first time.

PT says, "It's your first exploration of this world. That's why it's called the house of desires."

PT sPeaks of the PhacT that in today's age, the 3rd house relates to browsing and surfing on the internet. He also states that it is the house of writing as this activity involves some form of exploration. It is also the house of anything done with the hands such as painting, playing guitar, short messaging or computer gaming.

"Any kind of surfing in the virtual world
3rd house. It's a house people don't pay
much attention to whereas it's very
crucial in this day and age.

If you want to find out the right things,
you have to browse the right way to the
right thing.

The onus falls on you to find the
right things, no matter where you
are in the world. "

PT exPlains that the 3rd house is a crucial house, especially in the Present times because of what it represents. He says it rules all internet content and that one has to use the internet to search for the right things in life. One has to go to the right place in the right way as the internet offers so many options to choose from. Therefore one needs discrimination to choose wisely. PT exPlains that discrimination is related to another part of the horoscope.

He describes the 3rd house as

"the actual energy impulse activation of our basic desire to get to something"

or in more simple terms

"initiative"

In the horoscope, the desire triangle is formed by houses 3, 7 and 11 of which the 3rd house is the beginning spark of all desires.

PT adds that whilst a lot of people know that 3rd house relates to short journeys, they don't realize it is also related to browsing and surfing the virtual world. PT states that people don't understand the magnitude of importance this entails, just the Phact that people are supposed to be able to search and get to the right things on the internet.

He says that it is one's onus to get to the right things since the internet has been given to beings so they have a chance to "gno".

Beings cannot pretend that things are out of their grasp anymore. PT declares

"It is a level playing field"

PT PoinTs out that there is no search or research without the 3rd house, as it is the 8th house from the 8th house.

PT closes his discussion on the 3rd house with an

insightful correlation between the 3rd house and Krittika nakshatra (one of the 27 constellations that PT discusses in his book "The 27 Celestial PorTals" aka "The 27 Nakshatras").

He says Krittika nakshatra is highly related to the 3rd house being the 3rd nakshatra, and that understanding Krittika leads to an understanding of the 3rd house and vice-versa. The Krittika function that relates to cutting naturally applies to 3rd house activities. For example, when one decides to explore, it involves cutting out a lot of options in order to decide where, when and how to travel that journey.
PT says 3rd house activities require a lot of cutting out which is primarily Krittika's domain.

In this world of widespread confusion and conflicting opinions in astrology, we are very PhorTunate that PT brings so much clarity to this PhascinaTing discipline.

PT Mainstream

The most imPorTant book on the PlaneT : **"P's giTa – scriPTures for the now"** has recently been featured in over 500 news sites including:-

Yahoo News
Yahoo finance
Yahoo lifestyle
Fox News
Associated Press
The Times
Daily Herald
NBC
ABC
CBS Network
Google News

"Solutions to all world's problems in only one book.

PT aka Prashant Trivedi has penned a masterpiece that can enlighten humanity for generations to come. P's giTa has already been translated into 11 languages and represents the core essence of Vedic knowledge and wisdom for the present age. This is the world's most sacred scriptures compiled into its most condensed and lucid form to explain the ultimate truth about life and existence."

- Yahoo News

BeOmega were in the news this past month in more than a dozen journals & magazines including

Issuewire	Pause and Play
ANR Magazine	360 Media Hub
Fox News	Daily Tribune
The Star	NBC

"AS FAST AS YOU CAN: BEOMEGA ARE QUITE SUPERB ON THE GROOVY MODERN CLASSIC 'RETURN OF THE BIRDMAN'

Taken off their latest eleven-track album named 'Kalki – Return of The Birdman', BeOmega return with probably their best song yet with 'Return of The Birdman'.

BeOmega is a UK-based crop-circle-festival-playing three-piece psychedelic rock band who somehow morph the conscious world from their vivid imagination, into an exhilarating rock n roll experience like you have never heard before. They make that earthy sound that is rather rare, and feels like an outer body occurrence..."

by Llewelyn Screen, ANR Factory

New countries have been lucky enough to
recently benefit from PT's wisdom including
Albania, France, Spain, Argentina

COSMOLOGÍA VÉDICA
PROGRAMA: EL PORTAL

La Revolución holística del mundo Védico.
Entrevista a Prashant Trivedi

expoomline, Argentina

LIVE : Prashant Trivedi "Conscience divine pour
les temps modernes" + langue des oiseaux.

Prashant TriVedi on Radio Rilindja Oslo

Create & Submit your
own Praises online to
honor Divine 𝒫𝒯 at
Vedic.space

JUDGEMENT uPdaTe

Mankind is supposed to live aligned with Divine and Nature. However, during the last two decades, the disconnection between humans and nature has created major natural events which haven't been documented in the mainstream medias. Nonetheless, PhacTs remain that major natural disasters, such as earthquakes, floodings, storms, tsunamis, insect swarms, landslides, abnormal extreme weather changes and more, have been shaking the earth for a notable period of time now. PT has exhaustively documented those very pivotal events on his channel. Through these events, it is very easy to understand not only the PoTency of nature's Power, but also the Powerlessness of mankind in front of such enormous strength.

PT's playlist ~

"Judgement Day by the Real Avatar"

at You Tube Channel ~

"the PT Avatar "

is a strong testimonial of what is truly happening on our PlaneT.

When mankind's foolishness has gone so far it is only reasonable for Mother Nature to stop the foolishness of her children. The PhacT that PT, a being with tremendous gravity, has incarnated on Earth, greatly helps Mother Nature regain her balance. PT's incredible connection with nature is a great help. His Presence is not only a PhacTor in the rising consciousness of man but also in the interesting to note that the Hopi Indians had predicted such events. They described the coming of « the true Pahana » coinciding with what they described as « The Great Purification ».

These times are imPorTant, as the coming of the Avatar on Earth forces the Purification of this Plane. PT exPlains more about the Judgement in this video ~

"2020 ~ the imPorTance of this year ~ Prashant Trivedi"
(You Tube channel ~ PT sPeaks)

"20 is the number of Judgement" » PT

PT has stated many times that a Judgement is happening on this Earth. He gave special imPorTance to the year 2020 as it has two twenties in it. PT stated that the Judgement was going to be seen by the masses in 2020.

It is interesting to note that PT has been sPeaking about the Judgement since more than a decade. Even though people may have not realized that « the judgment is happening », PT declares, *"Everyone will get the feeling that something is happening"*. That statement stands true since mass consciousness has experienced even more chaos and suffering since the Covid-19 happenings.

*"The mainstream media will not cover natural disasters with any magnitude, (things which are happening by Nature and Divine) and they will try to distract the masses by focusing their attention on other things, making them look more important ,"*said PT.

PT adds that the masses will have to get to alternative media, but even in the mainstream, people will still get a picture of some judgement.

PT reassures that it is not the end of the world but simply a time where the Judgement becomes clear to the masses as a whole.

natural Corona (corona meaning halo)

A E I O U M

Real ॐ Revealed

in the Beginning arises the dot

the dot moves to create an arc (golden mean spiral!)

one becomes two

static & kinetic, Shiv & Shakti

three arcs are created with the dot in the center

Trinity is established

Multi-verse is born

AEIOUM is thus the symbol of creation

called Om or Aum when true knowledge is lost

amongst children of earth

every vowel is part of the play ...

66

Kalki - Return of the Birdman
by BeOmega

BEOMEGA TAKE YOU TO THE OUTER EDGE OF MUSIVERSE

from where arrives

kalki

return of the birdman

LIKE IT IS. LIKE IT will BE.

Available at Online Stores including Band CamP.

ditto.fm/kalki-return-of-the-birdman

beomega.bandcamp.com/album/kalki-return-of-the-birdman

Outer Edge of Musiverse

BEOMEGA TAKE YOU TO THE OUTER EDGE OF MUSIVERSE

**BeOmega show you the earth
the milky way & beyond**

LIKE IT IS. LIKE IT SHOULD BE

Available at Online Stores including Band CamP.

ditto.fm/outer-edge-of-musiverse

beomega.bandcamp.com/album/outer-edge-of-musiverse

Apps

Prash Time Wheel

Prash Time Wheel is a straightforward, free Jyotish/Vedic Astrology app to generate an accurate chart and Panchang for the present moment.
* Generate a chart to see which houses, signs and Nakshatras/Asterisms the Grahas/Planets are in at the current time.
* See the current Tithi/Moonphase.
* See the current Karna and Yoga.

Prash Nakshatra

This app puts the Vedic Wisdom of the 27 Nakshatras at your fingertips.
* Generate your birth chart.
* Find out which Nakshatras you have.
* Generate other people's birth chart.
* Learn about the Nakshatras as they appear in the sky, their meaning, functionings, professions, auspicious activities and much more.
* Get access to the timeless vedic knowledge by Prash Trivedi.
* Take it with you wherever you go.
* Ancient Vedic Wisdom with the functionality of a modern app.
* Send consultation request.

Prash Real Vedic Chart

Generate accurate Jyotish Vedic Horoscope / Birth Chart / Kundli. See Nakshatras and Panchang. Most importantly find out the Real accurate position of the Grahas (Planets) in your Real Bhav (House) Chart. No more confusion or choosing of different calculation parameters ! This is the only app which gives this info in a clear straightforward way. Consultation contact from inside the app.

Vedic Astrology Books

Available at rvaf.org & major stores like Amazon.com

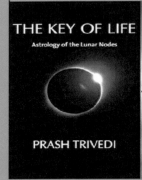

The Key of Life - Astrology of the Lunar Nodes

(aka "The Rahu Ketu Experience")

by Prash Trivedi

David Frawley, the well known Vedic scholar writes in his foreword ~

"Prash Trivedi, India's most insightful young astrologer offers what is probably the longest, most researched and most original book on Lunar Nodes (Rahu & Ketu in Vedic Astrology) published in modern times. This book is worthy of serious examination by all students of Astrology and all those interested in the great mysteries of life, death, karma and transformation."

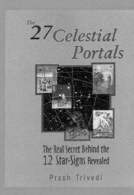

The 27 Celestial Portals
aka
"The Rahu Ketu Experience"

by Prash Trivedi

Prash Trivedi's book on nakshatras has no equal. It will open your mind to a new way to practice Vedic astrology, not just using nakshatras but understanding how these 27 segments of the zodiac transmit energy and awareness. This is the kind of information that only comes as a result of living a life that earns you the right to access higher knowledge.

The nakshatras, ancient in origin, can help you understand why each sunrise will bring something new into your life.

You Tube

Lotus Ocean

PT sPeaks

Game of Tones - Best Tones on the PlaneT!!!

The PT Avatar

BeOmega

P Places

Facebook

Prashant Trivedi

Prashant the Axis Trivedi

Lotus Ocean

Real Vedic Astrology Forum

Lotus Ocean
P's giTa ScriPTures for the now

BeOmega

Lotus Ocean Meditation

P Places

Websites

lotus-ocean.net

rvaf.org

osfa.org.uk

BeOmega.org

P Places

Patreon

patreon.com/lotusocean

ॐ Shri Ganeshaye Namah

ॐ Shri Durga MahaDevi Jagadambaye Namah

a "Lotus" arises in the dirty mud of this world -
sent from the divine realm above the celestial ocean
Everything is just 'Sound & Light' &
Everything's evolution is clear from its 'Sound & Light
to facilitate evolution through raising of vibrations...

all films are Live on locations around
bhudevi (earth goddess) & most of the Plays are done live & extempore by PT...